YOGA
FOR FUN!

by Jana Voelke Studelska

Content Adviser: Lorraine Shea, Executive Editor, FIT YOGA magazine, New York, New York
Reading Adviser: Frances J. Bonacci, Ed.D, Reading Specialist, Cambridge, Massachusetts

Compass Point Books ✦ Minneapolis, Minnesota

Compass Point Books
3109 West 50th Street, #115
Minneapolis, MN 55410

Visit Compass Point Books on the Internet at www.compasspointbooks.com
or e-mail your request to custserv@compasspointbooks.com

Photographs ©: WizData/BigStockPhoto, front cover (left); Svetlana Zhurkin, front cover (right); Junji Takemoto/iStockphoto, 4 (top); Anna Bryukhanova/iStockphoto, 4–5; The British Museum/Topfoto, 6, 42 (front); Everett Collection/Rex Features, 7 (top); Lisa Kyle Young/iStockphoto, 7 (bottom); Carson Zullinger, 8–9; Gustaf Brundin/iStockphoto, 10 (top); Koch Valérie/iStockphoto, 10–11; Ana Abejon/iStockphoto, 12–13; Ninoslav Dotlic/iStockphoto, 13 (right); The Image Works/Topfoto, 15; Phil Date/iStockphoto, 16; Suprijono Suharjoto/BigStockPhoto, 17; Rose Deakin/Topfoto, 19 (top); Yogamad.com, 19 (middle & bottom); Darren Green/BigStockPhoto, 20–21; Phil Date/iStockphoto, 21 (right); Rafal Gl bowski/iStockphoto, 22; Anness Publishing, 23, 33 (right), 34–35; Nataliya Verestoun/iStockphoto, 24–25; David Chang, 25 (right); Kateryna Govorushchenko/iStockphoto, 26; JinYoung Lee/BigStockPhoto, 27; Markus Seidel/iStockphoto, 28 (left); Lawrence Sawyer/iStockphoto, 28–29; Penny Burt/iStockphoto, 29 (right); Rex/Rex Features, 30–31; Fred Goldstein/iStockphoto, 32–33, 36–37, 38; Chris Stanbury/Topfoto, 37 (right); Greg Nicholas/iStockphoto, 39 (left); Stanislav Komogorov/iStockphoto, 39 (right); Nancy Rivera/Rex Features, 40; Paulus Rusyanto/iStockphoto, 41, 42 (back), 47; Bojan Tezak/iStockphoto, 43 (all); Ana Abejon/iStockphoto, 44 (all); KPA/HIP/Topfoto, 45.

Editors: Lionel Bender and Brenda Haugen
Designer: Bill SMITH STUDIO
Page Production: Ben White and Ashlee Schultz
Photo Researchers: Suzanne O'Farrell and Kim Richardson
Art Director: Jaime Martens
Creative Director: Keith Griffin
Editorial Director: Nick Healy
Managing Editor: Catherine Neitge
Yoga for Fun! was produced for Compass Point Books by Bender Richardson White, UK

Library of Congress Cataloging-in-Publication Data
Studelska, Jana Voelke.
  Yoga for fun! / by Jana Voelke Studelska.
    p. cm. — (For fun)
  ISBN-13: 978-0-7565-3282-6 (library binding)
  ISBN-10: 0-7565-3282-5 (library binding)
1. Yoga—Juvenile literature. I. Title. II. Series.
  RA781.7.S82 2008
  613.7'046—dc22   2007004769

This book was manufactured with paper containing at least 10 percent post-consumer waste.

Table of Contents

The Basics

INTRODUCTION / Ommmmmm 4

HISTORY / Ancient Start 6

WHY YOGA? / Move Your Body, Move Your Mind 8

THE SPIRITUAL SIDE / The Eight Limbs 10

KINDS OF YOGA / The Big Picture 12

SNEAK PEAK / Inside a Yoga Class 14

KEEP MOVING / Practice, Practice 16

Doing It

OFF YOU GO / Getting Started 18

SIT OR EASY POSITION / Sukhasana 20

CAT DOG / Bidalasana and Svanasana 22

MOUNTAIN / Tadasana 24

STANDING FORWARD BEND / Uttanasana 26

COBRA / Bhujangasana 28

SUN SALUTATION / Surya Namaskar 30

CORPSE / Shavasana 32

People, Places, and Fun

YOGA AND YOUTH / Yoga at School 34

YOGA, SPORT, STUDY, AND MUSIC / Happy Campers 36

OLD AND YOUNG ALIKE / Everyone Om! 38

THE RICH AND FAMOUS / Who Does Yoga? 40

TIMELINE / What Happened When? 42

TRIVIA / Fun Yoga Facts 44

● ●

QUICK REFERENCE GUIDE / Yoga Words to Know 46

GLOSSARY / Other Words to Know 47

WHERE TO LEARN MORE 47

INDEX 48

Note: In this book, there are two kinds of vocabulary words. Yoga Words to Know are words specific to practicing yoga. They are defined on page 46. Other Words to Know are helpful words that aren't related only to yoga. They are defined on page 47.

Ommmmm

Yoga is everywhere! Sailors on a Navy ship do yoga in their boots and uniforms. Movie stars and famous athletes talk about practicing yoga. At the mall, yoga fashions and colorful yoga mats are displayed in windows. In towns, yoga studios invite students to classes, where they learn to relax, concentrate, and breathe.

The word *yoga* comes from an ancient language called Sanskrit and means "union, or bringing together." Yoga brings together mind, body, and spirit. Those who practice yoga say they feel changes in their bodies and minds within minutes and deeper changes with regular practice. Yoga helps remind people of the energy and life that all humans share.

Om

Om is a mantra, a sacred, powerful sound and symbol with a vibration that is thought to be universal. In yoga, *om* is a sound that means "I am one with the universe."

People have been using yoga for thousands of years to feel healthy, relaxed, and happy. Its benefits have long been known in India and are studied by medical researchers.

Yoga is great exercise and makes people feel more energetic and peaceful. It's both playful and serious. It's a form of exercise you can practice all of your life.

Ancient Start

The Indus Valley, in present-day Pakistan, was home to an important ancient civilization. Finds in the area have given us clues about the origins of yoga. In two early cities, archeologists have found 5,000-year-old stone seals with images of yoga poses carved into the large surfaces.

Ancient texts from the Indus Valley —among the oldest written records in the world—refer to yoga. They tell beautiful stories that are still a part of Indian culture today.

The *Upanishads*, written around 800 B.C., contain songs, poems, and stories encouraging meditation, selfless action, and wisdom. These are the principles of yoga. The *Yoga Sutras* was written around 200 A.D. by a writer and philosopher named Patanjali. The *Yoga Sutras* includes eight steps—or paths of yoga—that are still the basis of yoga today.

Upanishads

The word *Upanishads* comes from *shad*, which means to sit, *upa* meaning near, and *ni* meaning down. This suggests that the only way a student could learn the truths hidden in its texts was to sit at the foot of a guru, or teacher.

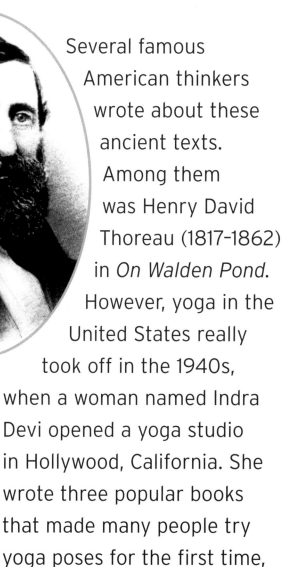

Several famous American thinkers wrote about these ancient texts. Among them was Henry David Thoreau (1817-1862) in *On Walden Pond*. However, yoga in the United States really took off in the 1940s, when a woman named Indra Devi opened a yoga studio in Hollywood, California. She wrote three popular books that made many people try yoga poses for the first time, including trying to stand on their heads in upside-down meditation!

Move Your Body, Move Your Mind

Pay attention to your breath, making it slow and deep. Pay attention to your posture, making it strong and purposeful. Pay attention to your mind, making it calm and focused.

Soon you'll realize that breath, posture, and mind are only the beginning of fun with yoga. You are a vast, powerful person with an energy flowing not only through you, but through all humans—and all through the universe. Exploring that amazing connection between mind and body is the goal of yoga. People report feeling stronger, more limber, and more flexible. They also report better feelings of inner strength, self-confidence, and concentration.

Musicians, dancers, and athletes find that yoga improves their performances.

Your body is changing, and yoga helps you understand all your parts and movements. As you grow, yoga keeps your body balanced, healthy, and strong. It also helps you with your schoolwork. To prepare for tests, try doing breathing exercises, and imagine yourself calm and focused just as in yoga class. In the middle of studying, try a few poses to get your mind going, and then get back to work.

People with health problems, such as cancer patients, use yoga to help their recovery. Busy people use yoga to calm their minds and relieve the stress of work.

The Eight Limbs

Yoga is not a religion. It is a tradition and belief. Yoga offers techniques, or tools, that anyone can use to add meaning to their lives. Yoga makes each person explore his or her own experience and helps people discover what is true and what works for them.

While yoga has no rules, there is a set of eight limbs, or principles, the *ashtanga*, which guides people toward using yoga to the fullest. Some people spend their whole lives studying these principles. Just learning about two of them, the *yamas* and *niyamas*, which are guidelines, codes, or morals by which to live, can take many years of study. In the United States, most people work on only three of the principles: *asana*, *pranayama*, and *dhyana*.

The Ashtanga

Yama: "Restraint" Five ethical rules

Niyama: "Observance" Five moral rules

Asana: Poses

Pranayama: Control of breath

Pratyhara: Union of senses and thought

Dharana: Deep concentration

Dhyana: Deep meditation

Samadhi: Awakening of spirit

11

The Big Picture

There are more than 100 different kinds of yoga. Each is unique, and each person who practices yoga experiences something different. Most people choose a style according to their needs, their body's health, or perhaps just by accident. In the end, however, all yoga works toward the same goals: the union of body, mind, and spirit.

In **kundalini yoga**, there is a great awareness of the spine. We know that our nerves travel up and down the spine. Kundalini yoga teaches that energy flows there, too. When energy is raised, many things change in our bodies and minds.

In **hatha yoga**, the focus is on long stretches and flexibility, with slow, deep breathing. This can be very soothing for the mind. This is the kind of mellow style most people think of when they picture yoga.

In India, yoga is a daily part of life. In the morning, it's common to see people performing the sun salutation, or *surya namaskar*, a set of poses and breaths dedicated to *surya*, the sun.

Ashtanga yoga is often called power yoga. Students do many *vinyasas*, a Sanskrit word for a series of flowing movements that warm up the body all over. This is a very active form of yoga. Students move quickly through poses, not holding them as long as in other styles. You'll sweat in this class!

Inside a Yoga Class

Do you wonder what a yoga class might be like? How to act? What to wear?

Make sure to dress comfortably. Most people like to wear cotton shorts or loose pants with tucked in T-shirts or tank tops that won't float over their heads when they're working. Yoga is always practiced barefoot, so don't worry about special shoes. Bring a water bottle. Yoga is thirsty exercise!

Yoga classes are for people of all ages and abilities. Don't think that you're too young, too old, too chubby, or too anything! Each body has its own challenges, and each body has its own strengths. Try sitting a few rows back so you can watch other students.

Each teacher has her or his own style. Some are playful. Some are serious. A good yoga teacher will always encourage you to modify postures to work for your body.

Namaste

In yoga, *namaste* (pronounced *nah-mah-STAY*) is used much the way *hello* or *goodbye* is used in English. Translated it means "the spirit in  me greets the spirit in you." It is a greeting that honors the sacredness and interconnection of everyone, as well as the source of that connection.

Practice, Practice

The more often you practice yoga, the better. Going to class once a week is great, but practicing at home three or four times a week is going to really change the way you feel.

Perfect Timing

If making time is a problem, try breaking it down. How about a few minutes before school and a few more minutes before bed? Or try a 10-minute yoga break while you're studying.

Some days yoga practice is just repetition. However, on other days, you'll find you learn something incredible about yourself or your body. As you advance, you can challenge yourself with more difficult poses and holding them longer.

There's a pose, a breath, a practice for every mood. It's fun to get beyond just doing the postures. Start thinking about what they mean. What does it feel like to be a cobra? If you're upset and frustrated, what can you learn and how can you benefit from the warrior pose?

You may want to try a yoga video. There are some great videos especially for beginners. A good plan is to do yoga routines with a friend so you can keep each other on track.

Getting Started

Just like finding balance in a yoga pose, you must find balance in yoga practice. Be kind to yourself, and listen to your body telling you what it likes and what hurts. Balance that message with the knowledge that yoga is about challenging yourself and your body.

Yoga is a gentle, individual sport. There is no competition. You don't win anything for doing a pose correctly or holding it longer than anyone else. In fact, if you push too hard, you won't enjoy yoga.

It's great to do yoga at home, but working with a teacher is best. Class is a great way to feel the "yoga vibe," to meet people, and to learn more. Plus, a teacher can help you adjust your poses to meet your body's needs.

A **yoga mat** gives you a stable, nonslip surface on which to do your poses. Most studios have mats for students to use during class. It's nice to have one of your own, for class and use at home.

Straps help you stretch your limbs and hold poses longer. Most come with buckles that adjust the strap's length. As you become more practiced, you might add sandbags to your straps to extend your stretches and challenge your muscles a litle more.

Blocks, wedges, bolsters, and blankets give support or lift. By making your pose more comfortable, these props keep your body aligned.

Sukhasana

Sukhasana helps strengthen your lower back, open your groin and hips, and slow your breathing.

1. The sitting position helps bring your awareness to your breathing and body. Often this *asana* is a starting position, done at the beginning of class.

2. Sit cross-legged with your hands on your knees. Focus on your breath, breathing in and out through your nose, slowly and fully. Keep your spine straight, and push the bones in your bottom down into the floor. Visualize your knees gently dropping lower. If you're uncomfortable, sit on a cushion or block, which will help support your back and hips. Take five slow, deep breaths.

Pronounced as *su-KAH-sa-na*.
Sanskrit translation: *Sukh* means to make happy.

Bidalasana and Svanasana

The cat and dog poses are opposites, each offering different gifts. Realize what each pose brings to your body.

1. On your hands and knees, put your hands just below and in front of your shoulders, with your legs about hip-width apart.

2. Inhale, dropping your back downward, so that your tailbone and pelvis tilt up and your head extends up. Let your spine curve down, dropping your stomach low.

Stretch gently. This is the dog position.

3. As you exhale, move into the cat position by reversing the arch of your spine. Tilt your pelvis down. Raise up your belly and chest into a curve. Make your head reach down toward the floor. Appreciate the difference from the dog pose.

Think how relaxed a cat and dog look when they relax.

4. Repeat several times, flowing smoothly from cat to dog, dog to cat.

This is really two poses, one flowing into the other as you repeat them.

Pronounced as *bee-dah-LAH-sa-na* and *sva-NAH-sa-na*.
Sanskrit translation: *Bidal* means cat; *svana* means dog.

Tadasana

Like a mountain, your body can experience being rooted firmly to the earth, steady and motionless.

1. Stand with your feet touching, from heel to big toe. Balance your weight evenly on both feet. Put your hands at your sides, your face and eyes forward. Make your spine very tall, as if the tip-top of your head were being pulled up by a string. Feel your heels, your feet, and your toes make contact with the ground. Slightly tighten your knees, thighs, stomach, and buttocks to hold a solid posture.

2. Breathe. As you inhale, imagine your breath coming up through the floor, rising through your legs, torso, and up into your head. Exhale your breath down

The *tadasana* helps you improve posture, balance, and brings self-awareness.

from your head, through your chest, stomach, and legs and out your feet. Hold the posture, but try not to tense up. Repeat five times.

3. On your next inhale, raise your arms over your head, and hold the pose for several breaths. Lower your arms on an exhale.

4. Try raising and lowering your arms with your breath: raise, inhale; lower, exhale. Repeat five times.

Pronounced as *ta-DAH-sa-na*.
Sanskrit translation: *Tada* means mountain, or standing firmly without moving.

Uttanasana

Each muscle stretches and each vertebrae moves with this asana. It also increases blood flow to the stomach and digestive organs.

1. Stand in tadasana, your back and head straight, shoulders level. Inhale, and stretch your arms overhead.

2. While exhaling, bring your arms out to your sides, and fold your body forward. Bring your arms over your head, and reach your hands to the floor.

3. Inhale slowly, and stretch your spine forward so your body is an upside-down "L" shape. Let your arms dangle straight down.

4. Exhale slowly, and bend forward at the waist until you can reach the floor with your hands. Bring your head down close to your knees while keeping your legs straight. Hold the pose until you are done exhaling.

5. Inhale as you slowly unfold and come up to stand with your arms overhead. Exhale, and bring your arms to your side. Repeat the entire cycle five times.

Bhujangasana

Bhujangasana strengthens your arms and wrists and stretches muscles in your chest. By holding the arch in your back, your stomach and pelvic muscles are strengthened. This *asana* also stretches and aligns your back and spine. Like a cobra, you are uncoiling yourself and your energy.

1. Lie down on your stomach, with your legs together and your toes pointed back. Pull your arms close to your body.

2. Inhaling through your nose, press your hands—palms down— on the floor. Slowly raise your head and chest off the ground as high as they will comfortably go. Squeeze your bottom muscles together tightly.

3. Keep your head up and chest out. From pelvis to toes, your body should be touching the ground. Stretch your spine forward, and bring your shoulders back.

4. Breathe carefully and slowly, several times, then gently release, letting your chest meet the ground. Relax with your arms at your side again, and repeat several times.

Surya Namaskar

This position stretches all your body muscles.

1. Stand with your feet together and hands in a
    prayer position at your heart. Breathing in, raise
    your arms above your head, and slowly stretch
    your spine into an arch.

2. Slowly breathing out, bend over, touching your
    fingers to your toes and your head to your knees.
    Don't worry if you can't reach.

3. Breathe in and take a big step back with your right
    foot while raising your head to look at the sky.
    You also bend your left knee, as if you are lunging
    forward. Make your right knee rest on the floor.

Pronounced as *SOOR-yee-ah NAH-ma-skar.*
Sanskrit translation:
Surya means sun;
namaskar means salute,
greeting, or praise.

4. Moving smoothly, bring your left foot back to meet with the other behind you, and push your back up into an upside-down "V." Make your head match the line of your arm.

5. Letting out your breath, lower your body to the floor, letting your forehead, chest, knees, and toes touch the ground. You should still have some tension, keeping your stomach and hips off the floor.

6. Breathe in slowly, arching your chest and spine back into a cobra pose. Breathe out, and bring your body back into the upside-down "V" pose.

7. Repeat first few movements and poses, but in reverse order: poses 4, 3, 2, 1.

Shavasana

Shavasana seems simple, but it is very challenging. Not only should your body be motionless, so should your mind. Like a motionless body, you are finding a deep and stable relaxation.

1. Lie flat on your back with your legs together but not touching and with your palms facing up. Keep your eyes gently closed.

2. Breathe deeply and slowly through the nostrils, letting your body sink into the ground. Focus your attention on the top of your head, and work your way down to your feet, bringing your mind to each part of your body, consciously relaxing it before going on to the next.

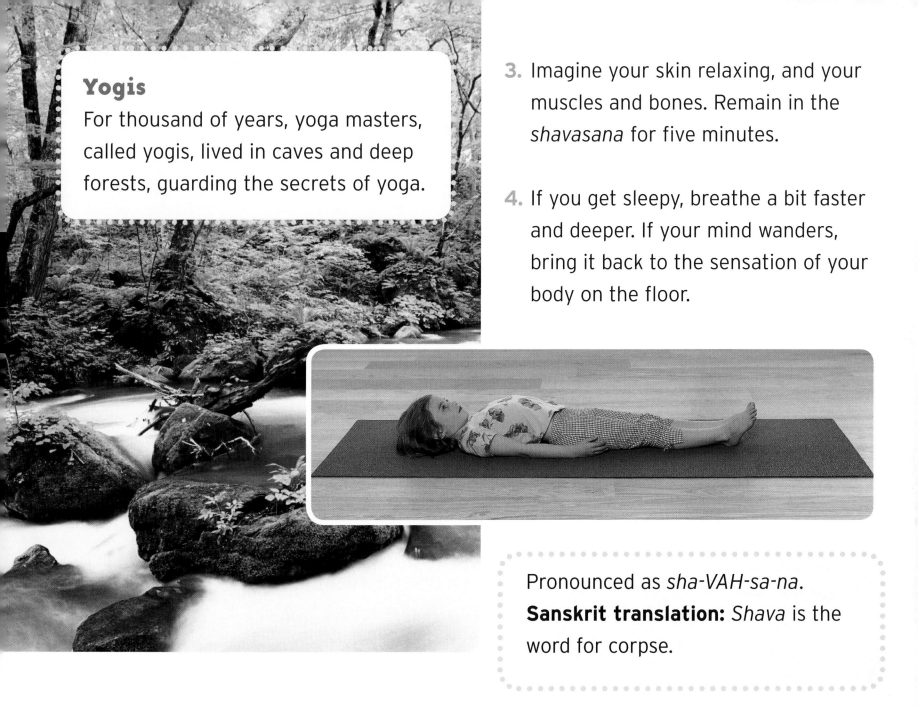

Yogis

For thousand of years, yoga masters, called yogis, lived in caves and deep forests, guarding the secrets of yoga.

3. Imagine your skin relaxing, and your muscles and bones. Remain in the *shavasana* for five minutes.

4. If you get sleepy, breathe a bit faster and deeper. If your mind wanders, bring it back to the sensation of your body on the floor.

Pronounced as *sha-VAH-sa-na*.
Sanskrit translation: *Shava* is the word for corpse.

Yoga at School

For 10 minutes, students concentrate on stretching, breathing in through their noses, and exhaling out through their mouths. The entire class lies quietly on the floor. The room is so quiet that everyone can hear the raindrops outside.

In some schools, yoga is a normal part of the day. Yoga is done in the classroom, in the gym, or outside on the lawn. Kids like it because they say it makes them feel calm and focused. Teachers like it for the same reason. In other schools, yoga is taught in gym class, just like swimming and tag football. It's a perfect addition to traditional sports, because it's noncompetitive but still uses both mind and body.

Young children who do yoga say it really improves their skills in other sports. The stretching, balance, and concentration from yoga are easy to apply to sports such as basketball or dance. Kids in music say the same thing. The breathing exercises really make a difference when blowing into a clarinet or singing a solo.

Young Yogi Kids

Kids are natural yogis. With such flexible limbs, they find it easy to get into poses and hold them. Active imaginations give kids an edge, too. Trying to be a cobra, uncoiling and lengthening, or a mountain, strong and rooted, makes kids' minds explode with ideas.

Happy Campers

Grab your sleeping bag and yoga mat! Summer's here, and it's time for yoga camp!

Across the country, some kids head off to yoga camp for a week of *asanas* and *pranayama* (poses and breath work), along with all the traditional camp activities, such as hiking, swimming, bonfires, and canoeing. One Massachusetts camp Web site says, "It's a week of healthy living, high thinking, and loads of fun!"

In Washington, D.C., kids can spend hot summer days in a cool yoga studio. For one or two weeks, students at a day camp combine yoga with crafts, journaling, and storytelling. They're home by their evening mealtime and back at camp each morning.

At the University of Arizona, a popular day camp for kids has combined chess camp with yoga camp. Yoga gets kids moving after a long morning of tournaments. It also helps those chess players to use their imaginations with chess strategies and to overcome stress.

Yoga Camp

Yoga camp is an excellent complement to sports, music, or academic camps.

Everyone Om!

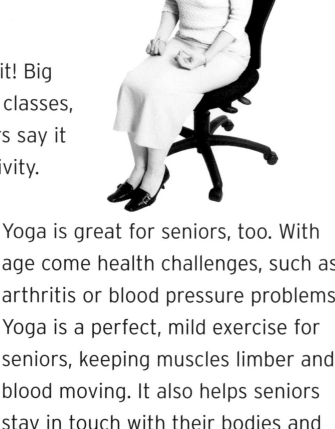

Is everyone a yogi? It sure seems like it! Big corporations offer employees free yoga classes, some of them right in the office. Workers say it relieves stress and boosts their productivity.

Pregnant women really benefit from yoga. It's not hard to imagine how a big, round belly could throw off your balance. And knowing how to meditate helps moms get through the hours of active labor. After the baby is born, mama and baby yoga classes help young families find ways to soothe cranky infants.

Yoga is great for seniors, too. With age come health challenges, such as arthritis or blood pressure problems. Yoga is a perfect, mild exercise for seniors, keeping muscles limber and blood moving. It also helps seniors stay in touch with their bodies and learn to deal with changes that are sometimes hard to accept.

Even at-risk youths are finding yoga. In several cities, volunteer instructors help those who normally couldn't afford yoga classes. In addition to building breath awareness and strength, they try to foster confidence, self esteem, stress relief, and empowerment.

Who Does Yoga?

Lots of famous movie and music stars are yoga fanatics. Among them are Madonna (right), Sting, and Sarah Jessica Parker.

But did you know that in Washington, D.C., in the gym of the Supreme Court, judges and staff may take classes every Tuesday morning? Justice Sandra Day O'Connor, who retired from the court in 2006, was especially interested in yoga.

Kareem Abdul-Jabbar, the Los Angeles Lakers' basketball star, practiced yoga throughout his career.

New York Mets pitcher Orlando Hernandez is also a yoga student.

Surfer Emma Graham, who won several international competitions, does yoga. Opera star Robert Merrill loved yoga and shared it with many of his co-stars. Wimbledon tennis champion Maria Sharapova says yoga was part of her game.

Yoga Sells

Recently yoga and famous people doing yoga have been used to sell sports drinks, skin products, and even cars. But yoga isn't about fame, special clothes, or where you live. It's about being content with yourself, which is perhaps what attracts famous people to yoga in the first place!

41

What Happened When?

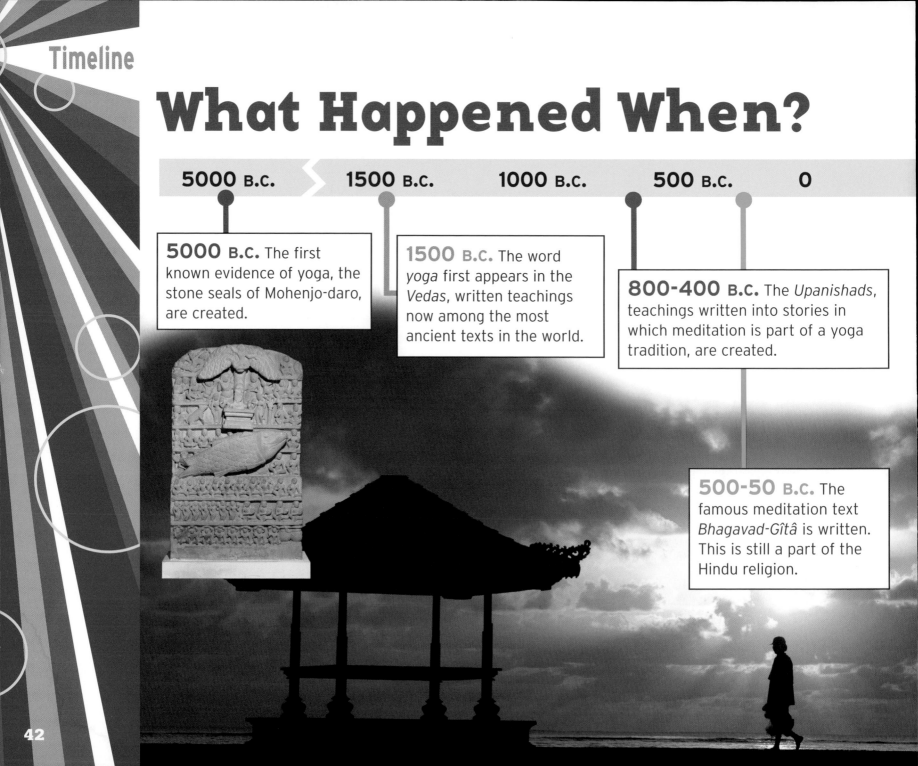

5000 B.C.   1500 B.C.   1000 B.C.   500 B.C.   0

5000 B.C. The first known evidence of yoga, the stone seals of Mohenjo-daro, are created.

1500 B.C. The word *yoga* first appears in the *Vedas*, written teachings now among the most ancient texts in the world.

800-400 B.C. The *Upanishads*, teachings written into stories in which meditation is part of a yoga tradition, are created.

500-50 B.C. The famous meditation text *Bhagavad-Gîtâ* is written. This is still a part of the Hindu religion.

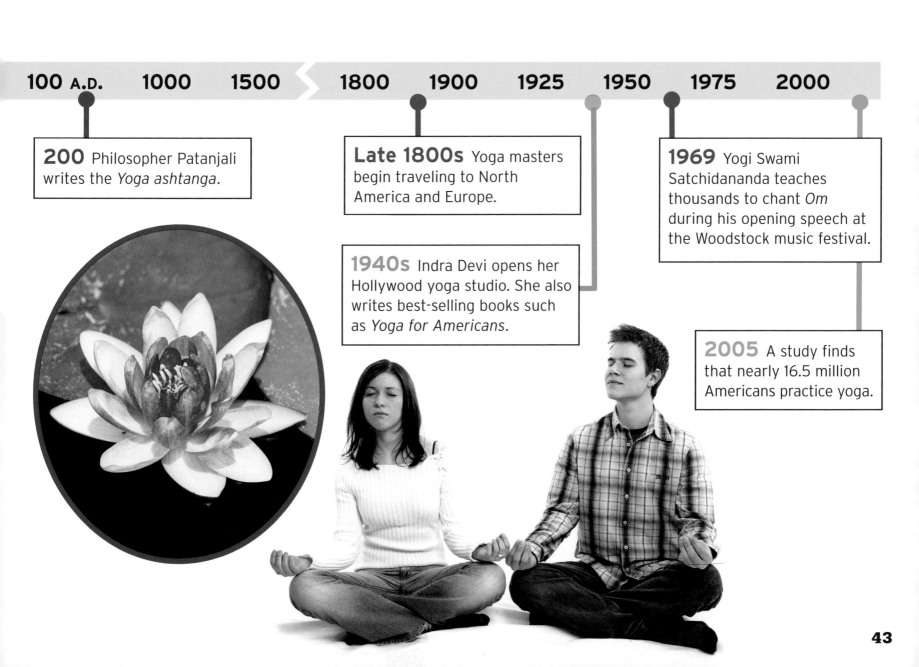

100 A.D.   **1000**   **1500**   **1800**   **1900**   **1925**   **1950**   **1975**   **2000**

200 Philosopher Patanjali writes the *Yoga ashtanga*.

Late 1800s Yoga masters begin traveling to North America and Europe.

1969 Yogi Swami Satchidananda teaches thousands to chant *Om* during his opening speech at the Woodstock music festival.

1940s Indra Devi opens her Hollywood yoga studio. She also writes best-selling books such as *Yoga for Americans*.

2005 A study finds that nearly 16.5 million Americans practice yoga.

Fun Yoga Facts

Indra Devi, who made yoga famous in the United States, was born Eugenie Peterson in Riga, Latvia. In 1927 she moved to India and acted in a film. She played the role of Indra Devi, a name she used for the rest of her life. In the 1940s she opened a Hollywood yoga studio. She died in 2002 at age 102.

Seva is a kind of yoga that is about volunteer work and the community. Rather than focusing on the body, seva yoga is about understanding the needs and wishes of others and confronting things that make us uncomfortable.

Cirque du Soleil is a theater group featuring jugglers, dancers, and contortionists, The theater performers often practice yoga. Contortionism is different from yoga. In yoga, the aim is the effect the posture has on mind and body. Contortionism is concerned only with posture.

In the 1960s the world-famous pop group the Beatles went all the way to India to learn yoga from the Maharishi Mahesh Yogi. Many of their fans took up yoga when they learned the Beatles were practicing. You can hear a sitar, a stringed instrument popular in India, in their song *Love You Too*.

Yoga Words to Know

asana: postures or poses of yoga

dharana: deep concentration in yoga

dhyana: deep meditation in yoga

guru: spiritual teacher or leader

kundalini: energy in each of us that can be awakened through yoga

mantra: sacred sound or phrase chanted during yoga. "Om" is a popular mantra

meditation: allowing the body to be consciously relaxed and the mind to be calm and focused

pranayama: breathing exercises of yoga

pratyhara: focusing of the mind in yoga

samadhi: awakening of the spirit in yoga

Sanskrit: ancient language of India and surrounding areas

sutra: Sanskrit word for "thread." A sutra is a written teaching.

vinyasa: sequence or flow of asanas linked by breath

yogi: person who follows the teachings of yoga

Other Words to Know

exhale: breathe out

focus: concentration of energy or attention on something

inhale: breathe in

pose: a certain way of holding your body

posture: much like a pose; the arrangement of your body and limbs

stress: tension or strain in your emotions or your body

universe: the place in which we exist, together with all the energy and matter within it

Where to Learn More

AT THE LIBRARY

Caldwell, Michaela. *The Girls' Yoga Book: Stretch Your Body, Open Your Mind, & Have Fun*! Toronto, Ont.: Maple Tree Press, 2005.

Luby, Thia. *Yoga for Teens: How to Improve Your Fitness, Confidence, Appearance, and Health–And Have Fun Doing It!* Santa Fe, N.M.: Clear Light Publications, 2000.

ON THE ROAD

Discovery Yoga
3 Davis St.
St. Augustine, FL 32084
904/824-7454

ON THE WEB

For more information on this topic, use FactHound.

1. Go to *www.facthound.com*
2. Type in this book ID: 0756532825
3. Click on the *Fetch It* button.

FactHound will find the best Web sites for you.

INDEX

Asana, 10, 11, 20, 28, 36
Ashtanga, 10, 11, 13, 43

Beatles, 45
Bhujangasana, 28–29
Bidalasana, 22–23
Blankets, 19
Blocks, 19, 20
Bolster, 18, 19
Breath, Breathing, 4, 8, 9, 11, 12, 13, 17, 20, 24, 25, 31, 35, 36, 39

Cat and Dog pose, 22–23
Cobra, 17, 28–29, 31, 35
Concentration, 8, 11, 35

Devi, Indra, 7, 43, 44
Dhyana, 10, 11

Energy, 4, 8, 12, 28
Exercise, 5, 9, 14, 35, 38

Guru, 7

Hatha yoga, 12
Health, 5, 9, 12, 35, 38
Hollywood, 7, 43, 44

India, 5, 13, 44, 45
Indus Valley, 6

Kundalini yoga, 12

Meditation, 6, 7, 11, 42
Mind, 4, 8, 9, 12, 26, 32, 33, 34, 35, 45

Namaste, 15
Niyamas, 10, 11

Om, 5, 43

Patanjali, 6, 43
Posture, 8, 14, 17, 24, 25, 45
Power yoga, 13
Pranayama, 10, 11, 36
Pratyhara, 11

Samadhi, 11
Sandbag, 18, 19
Sanskrit, 4, 13, 21, 23, 25, 27, 29, 31, 33
Seva, 44
Shavasana, 32–33
Shoes, 14
Spine, 12, 20, 22, 24, 28, 30, 31
Straps, 18, 19
Stress, 9, 38, 39
Sukhasana, 20–21
Sun salutation, 13, 30–31
Surya Namaskar, 13, 30–31
Svanasana, 22–23

Tadasana, 24–25
Thoreau, Henry David, 7

Upanishads, 6, 7, 42
Uttanasana, 26–27

Vinyasas, 13

Warrior, 17
Water bottle, 14
Wedges, 19

Yamas, 10, 11
Yoga camp, 36–37
Yoga mat, 4, 19, 36
Yoga Sutra, 6
Yogis, 33, 35, 38

ABOUT THE AUTHOR

Jana Voelke Studelska lives in northern Minnesota with her family, where she loves to garden, ski, read, and canoe. In addition to writing, she works as a midwife, with a busy homebirth practice.